@cheerially

This Small Moment's Shelter

By Imogen Scott

Don't you just love a free book.

Enjoy! xxx

This Small Moment's Shelter
© 2025 Imogen Scott
All rights reserved.

No part of this publication may be reproduced, distributed, or transmitted in any form or by any means, including photocopying, recording, or other electronic or mechanical methods, without the prior written permission of the author, except in the case of brief quotations used in reviews or scholarly works.

First Edition, June 2025
Self-published by Imogen Scott
Printed in United Kingdom
ISBN: 9798282330229

Table of Contents

1. *Hungover*
2. *Swallow*
3. *Absolution*
4. *Orange*
5. *Pastiche*
6. *Plum*
7. *Thread*
8. *Hoof*
9. *Life*
10. *Abyss*
11. *Salt*
12. *Full Circle*
13. *Flurry*
14. *Each Other*
15. *Sea Level*
16. *Travel*
17. *A Whale of a Time*
18. *The Attic Space*
19. *Concrete*
20. *Echo*
21. *Refuge*
22. *The Chaos Machine*
23. *Moonshine*
24. *Traffic*
25. *Entanglement*

26. Divided
27. Choices
28. Kismet
29. Conspiracy
30. Oblivion
31. Negative Entropy
32. Lily
33. Database
34. Tempus
35. Physics
36. Join
37. Feather
38. A Guide to Being Strong
39. Soundwave

To my mum, whose own words lit a path for mine.

"And fastened to a dying animal,

It knows not what it is..."

—W. B. Yeats, *Sailing to Byzantium*

Give to the birds what we can't eat, and by that, I mean our bones. Give to the fishes what we can't stomach, and by that, I mean our words. Give to the earth what we can't carry, and by that, I mean our souls.

Hungover

I want to be wanted,
forever and always, and
I want to drink.
To glimpse that sight behind the eyes,
that time does not matter,
because you can feel the present between your fingers,
and it is submissive,
yielding to the touch of the desperate,
and the needy, when it is so very needed
for it to listen to me,
this one and only time.
when I am asking for recognition from the universe:
that I am an old thing,
in the body of something very young.
And when I sit on the bench in the park,
I can feel the thumping of cogs
hollow out the space in which we live.
And yet,
we throw the ball,
and climb the trees,
and hold each other's hands,
regardless.

Swallow

It's all so dirty,
the act of living.
To lick the taste of it
off someone else's brow
and to call it love.
To kneel down in the dirt and grow
the thing we hold between
our teeth and chew,
bite down hard and swallow.
To wash our hands of the guilt
in a body of water that remembers
all that passes through it.
Running to the coast, just to breathe
in something fresh and raw.
To remember that we are creatures
and the filth of it is where we will
all return.
To remember that
someone is counting:
the seconds, the hours, the eyes
you meet and turn away from.
Counting the glasses of wine you drink,
and the words that trickle over.
Counting the times you have grovelled,
the times you have sworn off,
and pulled closer,
felt the underbelly
of a docile beast,
and carried the feeling of it home.

Absolution

Have you ever held the ocean in your hand,
hovering just above the surface of it,
water crashing against your palm.
The heavens have opened
and you have been found
wanting.

Have you not felt the urge
to lean back and give in,
to float across the waves,
to kill the fight against the natural order,
the slow progression,
the march toward the inevitable return
to the place of conception,
deep inside the hollows of an earth
that knows more than us
about the fated things
we try to push back against.

I want to feel safe and held,
and rattled to the core.
This is what we have to lose.

Orange

Hold the image of it still
and breathe in.
It seemed, in the quiet seconds of a minute
coming to a close,
that maybe you could understand it —
threads woven into a pattern just for us — a treat.
As if the clouds themselves had a purpose,
holding the colours of the many
and the truth of a few.
Striking orange,
the tang of a touch that lingers,
then squeezes tight the last few drops
of something sickly sweet and toxic.

Pastiche

I want to impress you without leaving an impression.
A glimmer of a reflection in glass that blinds you,
a second of light that catches you off guard
before the car reverses out of the driveway.

The brain is reacting to our lives,
taking note of it,
in streams of neurons like nets;
the small fingers of a child stretching out
to form a cat's cradle, a catch-all.

I am not sure where they are stored,
but when I move, they rattle:
small hardcopies of moments past.

How can something have felt so brief,
but be replayed as infinite?
Not necessary, nor impossible,
but alive and awake,
an eye staring out into full sun,
wishing it could blink.

Stuck, imagining contingencies,
the two of us in new roles:
one where I am capable,
and you are kind.

Plum

Nothing is certain,
and yet I know the colour
of something bruised
coalesces around the shade of purple.

Sanguine in hue,
the flush left behind,
where pain
was never meant to root.

A vein made
to channel and feed,
interrupted where the vessel
meets blunt force.

What if I get what I want,
but I had to beg to get it?
What if you get what you want,
and what you wanted was me begging?

What if your favourite colour is purple,
and I am the bruised thing,
willing to keep shedding?

What if the moment is a mirror,
reflecting an ellipsis
where neither of us say our peace.
Instead we remain stuck in motion,
running parallel,
a single sharp claw reaching out
to drag across our sides,
a reminder that some things are meant to sting?

And you are watching,
on the other side of a screen,
thinking what it would be like to stop,
if it wasn't so fun to witness,
and so gratifying to feel,
an animal loving the thing
it puts into its belly in order to survive.

Sustenance —
feeding each other in different ways,
fruits of our labour,
but we are both the tree and the seed,
the provider and the promise.

Thread

More familiar with the edge of a razor blade
than any form of consistency
that would lead me to renounce it;
a red thread pulled across skin,
so captivating because it is so pure.
Show me something that bleeds,
and I will believe it.

A form of proof as irreproachable
as a seal from our makers,
God, or the thing that pulls together atoms.
An executive mission coming from within:
cells willing to conform in order to persist.
Life,
and we cut it up in order to feel it,
in order to conquer it.

The other side of joy is a pain so deep
it wraps back around and makes you feel present,
like you could hold the moment if it would only just let you,
a tangible resistance, an elastic band snapping back
to remind you, you are real.

Coagulating into routine to protect
against the threat of novelty and the exhilaration of addiction.
A thread, like a snake wrapping around a cardinal sin,
but it's sometimes
ever so inviting.

Hoof

Having skin in the game
means giving yourself entirely to it
and I have said as much already.
Every inch, stapled with a price
I pay biweekly
in exchange for soft reminders
that I exist.

I'm writing to it,
like a stampede hurtling toward a cliff,
it always knew was coming.
Still, an ache urges each beast forward,
unwilling to relinquish the sight
of something that promises exhilaration.
Or perhaps it is about fear,
I forget.

An animal –
all hooves, all fur, all deep breaths –
rumbling into the space ahead
with the stride of a creature
terrified,
yet certain.

I would rather fall than turn back now,
for what else is the cost of stopping
but being forgotten?
And the body knows it,
resistant,
even as it pulls away.

But it does fade,
and we blame no one for it.

Time, the salve for eons of small footnotes,
hiccups in what was meant to be.
Anger was made to push us
through the first few steps,
until we can stumble toward desolation,
then collapse into acceptance
and lie still.

Life

So here it is, ripe and ready
for the taking,
the truth of the beast nestled tight inside its belly.
You just have to reach in, and
grab it.
What have you got to lose?
A hand,
perhaps even two,
and after that,
those pearly whites will do.
You just have to taste it.
The sharpness of the very letters
that curve around the feel of it.
It's not temptation;
it's the snap of an instinct coming home,
vengeance for the life you took
curled around forefinger and thumb,
bending chaos around the seconds
that trickle out like branches.
Do you not see?
Do you not understand?
We are sleeping soundly beneath it,
then sometimes breathing loudly above it,
arms outstretched wide just to touch it.
Then there's a sudden pull,
and it all collapses.

Abyss

If you think about it
for more than a couple of minutes,
it starts to get scary,
and I think that's okay.

When I was first told
that the deepest point of the ocean
was 36,000 feet,
I thought that fact would trouble me
far more than it ever did.

I thought it would come to affect me
in some dreadful, daunting way
I hadn't yet imagined.

As if to grow up
you had to swim down there
and touch the bottom.
Or that one day I'd find myself trapped,
drowning,
chased to the lowest point on earth,
where light doesn't even shine,
and find it familiar.

It began, as it often does,
a recurring thought curling
through my mind like smoke.

I'd stand on a sand dune
watching one blade of marram grass
push through the harsh terrain,
and I'd think about the simplicity
of unknown things.

I'd think about how I'll never know
what my father's hands looked like at twenty,
never know the boy he was
before the weight of the years settled in.

I'd think about how I'll never know
what real silence feels like,
without the chatter of the moment
pressing down on it.

I'd think about how I'll never know
what an atom truly is,
or the force that holds us together like glue,
millimetres away from touching.

These things exist quietly in the background
like flies,
little fruit flies bred from something rotten
or overripe —
the ones that float around your head,
occasionally buzzing past your ear.

You can hear the sound of the ocean
if you put a seashell to your ear,
but you can also hear it
in the rustle of duvet covers
and the low hum of a nearby train.

It's the sound of something crashing,
of one force hurtling towards another,
the sound of something relentlessly promising
to be nothing less than what it set out to be.
Sometimes it's as simple as that.

Somewhere, a small octopus is hiding in a shell,
waiting to do what it has always done.
And somewhere, a lone turtle is swimming
further out
than it has ever before,
born of sand just three days prior.

Somewhere, creatures
we cannot even see
are beginning to take shape,
floating in ways we could only wish to —
thoughtless, effortless, free.

Standing there, so close to the water,
I can't help but think
of all the things I can't see,
and don't understand,
and wish I did.

I used to watch my mother swim
these great long lengths across the bay,
and occasionally she would stop and float.
When I asked her why she did this,
she would tell me she was trying to be at peace,
and I didn't understand that she meant
at peace with all the things she'd already done
and all the choices she'd already made.

Out of all the things the ocean holds,
I've always been sure it harbours god.
That between each wave there is a gap
and that is where it dwells.
After all, that is where life came from.

Bubbling below the surface,
we rose from the sea,
we didn't descend from the sky.
And there is something far more primitive,
and ancient,
in the thought of us coming
from sea foam and salt,
born of water.

A murky process taking place
below the depths,
wholly unclear
in the muffled silence.

Life was not created,
that feels far too clean.
Life was brewed,
at the bottom of the ocean in the darkness —
perhaps 36,200 feet deep, to be exact.
We struggled for life.

If our Father was chance, luck, a flicker of light,
then our Mother was pure grit:
determination, hardship, perseverance.
A force of nature, throughout the ages,
bellowing through time, relentless.

I often say I don't know what it's like to be alive,
as if I'm not orchestrating a billion cells
that have been circulating,
recycling themselves,
since energy itself first exploded out of a thought,
a star,
a start of something.

I often say that I don't know what it's like to be alive,
as if I weren't also in some way the creature
at the bottom of the ocean.

A little creature,
with a little soul of its own.
Not Life with a capital L, but life —
the soft, quiet, inhale and exhale of a thing,
one thing after another,
after another,
after another.

Salt

I have felt the cold
of the ocean
on a hot summer's day,
and decided to keep swimming.
To let it momentarily
pull the air from my lungs,
and give back to me
in other ways.
The fear of what lies beneath my feet,
a depth as plunging
as a promise,
striking chords
only an animal of love
would yield to.
To not be pulled down,
submerged,
to not give in to the desire:
how it would feel to settle
between the waves,
and make a home there,
to give over to a power,
surely wiser,
the control of your body.

Full Circle

You cannot have the world
and eat it too.
Somewhere in between,
you must let go
of the fast and vicious thoughts
that snake around the fist
that keeps on reaching for more.

At some point, there is a voice that says:
Stop.
Caress instead the hollow space between each rib,
and fill it with earth —
rich, sodden soil —
and lie down flat,
and dream.

Flurry

Isn't it enough that you saw it?
The inkling of something,
a flurry of the great big thing.
The behind-the-scenes of how light is made,
between the branches of something growing, and strong, and living.

You, behind the helm of the sun,
each wave a catapult into the time it takes
for me to remember why
we are coursing through this together.

We talk about it in halves,
because there's a side that we do not understand
and one that we rage against.

It's on the tip of your tongue,
the promise of a life where each moment bleeds,
screaming to be seen,
like a pressure on your chest.

There'll be plenty more days,
but there will never be enough.

Each Other

The silence at night,
above the horizon or below the sea,
will remind you of an end
that stalks like a blessing,
ushering in stars that come and go,
from and of themselves,
in an expansive world we understand little of,
beyond the numbers that spell out a resting place
we will all one day come to know.

But meanwhile, here we are,
amidst the churning,
eating and feeding and loving and caring,
and growing and giving,
and taking back the seconds that were gifted to us,
when something came to,
through a long and heavy darkness,
to give you light.

Tailored at either end with an isolation
that shrinks every time you hold my hand.

Sea Level

The belly of a boat
hatches intimacy caught between
the breadth of space.

The window, half sky, half water,
split to inverse a world
where threats bubble up from below.

A vacuum is created,
a black hole, no noise, no matter,
no nothing but the lull of time
thrumming on like it always has.

And, when it tires,
the rupture will be sudden,
but this will stay the same,
stitched into memory
that belongs to neither of us
but instead to the tapestry of something bigger.

A something that promises to capture truths
that move in shallow patterns
like whirlpools.

Travel

Nighttime is the natural state of the universe,
and only when something ignites
can we see the soft edges
of atoms come together,
recognisable as home.
Somewhere for the sheep to graze,
for the sun to rise,
for the trains to shoot across the countryside,
bound for familiar places.
The slope of the land,
leading us to where
the water within us
wishes to settle.

A Whale of a Time

When I need a good shaking up,
I think of the whale,
with its mouth open wide.
And I think of the krill that do not see the beast,
but only feel the pull of it,
drawing them in.
The bristle of something down their backs,
and then a void that is as inviting
as a belly that groans for them.

How it must be similar for us,
when the tide of our life
recedes.
Kicking below the surface against machinations
that are older and stronger
than we think ourselves wise.
A pocket of air that shrinks
the moment down
to the absolute.

We will all be swallowed whole by time,
the great cosmic whale,
with its mouth open wide,
for us.

The Attic Space

Held up by the strength of years of trial and error,
a skeleton, an architecture, an archetype,
for the bodies that have come and gone,
and those that have still yet to tread
on the familiar soils of a trusted planet,
a fragile thing,
a home,
a growing green creature we dissolve into and seed from.
In a cycle that haunts us and drives us
and shelters us from the horrors of the endless and
the incomprehensible seconds that eclipse into light.
Just the one,
the one that counts:
the big-sounding noise that crashes from the attic above the universe
and tells us our time is up.

Concrete

Pale in comparison,
to the songs I heard growing up,
of the crickets at dusk,
or the pigeons at dawn,
somewhere
nested in the woods.
To curl beneath the moon,
and wake to its pastels.
To grow up,
a starfish on the sand,
drinking in the sun.
Yet,
the river sometimes speaks
so softly against the banks of the city,
I could reach down
and stroke it.

Echo

Do you think they can remember it,
the atoms — the brimming of the is,
without definition, without words?
The whirring, on and on and on,
of the right here, right now,
right there, right then.
Clinging to simple forms in the soft static
of a silence we come from and will return to.

We do not need to fear it;
the stars are shining so bright,
and being sucked in is as
natural as a deep breath,
settling into our lungs
and we have been doing that
since the very beginning.

When you pull skin taut,
scars begin to disappear.
And so the universe does the same,
stretching out to afford us
the privilege of time as a healer.

And when we find one another again,
when all of this folds back into itself,
it will not matter.
It will be one big jumble,
and all these words will just be a
small, quiet sound, like a hum,
the promise of
What if? Again?

Refuge

How many times,
do you pick up
and then put down,
the shell you use
to call home to the ocean.
In my mothers' room,
it sat on the top shelf,
and I would reach for it
on the weekends to hear its
quiet rushing. Secrets whispered
on a wind that blew from the coast.
Tucked away in the crevices
of an ancient cousin of itself.
Oh, how we keep safe
within ourselves,
the sounds of the places we have been.

The Chaos Machine

Starting with the touch of a sound
from the inside of a belly,
stretching out into space,
a starfish reaching out
to hug the advent of time.

You are, where you started off:
somewhere dark, somewhere familiar.

Knuckles closing around a thumb
that promises to play out a role that is co-created.
Clothes fit from genes that are hand-me-downs.
Eyes looking out onto a world
that is new to the both of us now.

Potential, like static left behind,
serves as a reminder and a warning,
that what attracts also crackles and shocks.

Two steps into a world handcrafted from chaos,
exempt from all jury,
we make of energy, a cascade:
patterns from the thoughts
about where we have come from,
and where we are going.
Disorder from the actions
that it takes for us to get there.

Moonshine

You say the wrong thing
to the crickets at dusk,
and they chirp a little louder,
in order to say:
it's okay,
we didn't hear you,
could barely understand you.
But have you seen the moon?
She's rising from her slumber to the east,
and the colours of the sky
are fighting to make space for her,
a cosmic swirl,
all so unlikely to be here,
even more so to be able to say,
Look at it, look at it all,
My god.

Traffic

A swarm of starlings
is not a whole, but at its core
just the movements of a few,
tracing through, across a net,
to create something more than itself.

A bird, just the one,
watching the other,
who watches another,
who twists, and folds, and
swerves, until there is a pattern among the many.

A moving thing, blind to itself,
except the feathers of its kin
at its side.

Entanglement

The people you love most
were the atoms you were near
in the creation of the universe.
Or, in other words...

You are as familiar to me as a turn of phrase,
the feel of autumn rushing to like dew,
the dull light of dawn just breaking,
offering us a sliver of an orange,
that bleeds out throughout the day.

In sum, it is all the things I feel
in the animal part of my brain,
nestled in the crest of it,
like a switch, a giving in,
to a thirsting compulsion,
to lay down and stay very still.

We are mechanical in our movements,
yet I watch yours like the trickle of a river,
whirring on,
wanting, waiting to reach out and touch the muscle of it.

Where the earth begins, is where you end,
and still, I'm sure the crickets call to us in their song,
little legs chirping by the lake, or out on the porch.
Moving through this small window of moments,
after so long apart.

We are as old as the time it took to recollide,
before what tore us from the energy we once were,
before we could speak of what haunts us now —
your heart, your lungs, your health —
a love that does not waver, but shall pass, and be passed on.

Divided

I feel my time is limited,
and sometimes feel the brush of it behind me,
like a hand reaching across a divide.
I was told it was a thin veil,
a sheet in the wind, hung up to dry,
and you are standing behind it.

Choices

Noble are the causes that rouse the many,
a cry like a strike of lightning in the night
that illuminates the room you're in, sleeping.

Delicate are the causes that whisper to the few,
like a symphony in the sound of silence,
deep in a forest, the trees a buffer
to the impertinence of life.

It does not stop, but when you try to
hold it still, I promise it will yield:
the universe folding away
into a snow globe.

In your hands,
and you can watch it,
shake it, and it will respond;
it's all up to you.

Kismet

Your lot in life,
is a series of misfortunes.
You think aloud to the morning
of a new dawning year.
Time has been quickening of late,
against the pulse of something
slowing down.
I want to think of life,
as the soft tendrils of a seedling,
ringlets of potential, twining
around a destiny –
your one and only fate.
On this fresh day,
as old as existence itself,
there has been a rushing of energy,
that you do not always see,
all so you'd find yourself here.

Conspiracy

There are many decisions you make in life.
You make the right one,
then you make the wrong one
as part of a conspiracy theory
that you are just a moving body,
one that is being pushed forwards;
and everything that is,
already was,
and always has been.

Things come together
in the same way they come undone,
at the seam,
the hollows of the joints,
the crevices foreboding a divide.
Somewhere between being seen
and being misunderstood.

Somewhere, you're standing in front of it all,
saying, please.
I have stumbled through
to tell you that a captive audience
is just a liability.
That I once filled those veins
with the blood you now spill.
And that we are always just a stone's throw away
from reaching the end of this small moment's shelter
before the big infinity begins.

Oblivion

You must know when you're dying,
there must be a shakiness in your chest,
or alarm bells that set off a sequence in your brain.

An all-hands-on deck,
spread of chemicals telling you
to reach out and hold on,
or to recoil inwards and breathe,
breathe,
keep breathing,
until something stops.

That something:
the heart,
or the blood through the vessels,
or the last action potential firing
across the branch of a neuron,
heading home,
a current short-circuiting itself into an oblivion
that starts with a small, resolute crack.

Negative Entropy

Four seconds before the end of the world,
and I choose to pray,
the pressure of both hands pressed together,
creating a steeple of my own design.

I choose to assert order over a sure thing,
and draw from within the last biological truth,
etched into small, vibrating organisms like a cry.

It tells me to trust,
in the face of the uncertainty folding over us
like a shadow,
one that has haunted the corners of the world
since the first bubble appeared.

It tells me to reach out,
to search for patterns,
to cycle back through the eras of data,
to find the right chain of events.

It tells me to see meaning,
like how there is something to be said
about the way we use our hands,
and how we always have done.

A lot of being alive is reaching for things,
palm outstretched, *please.*

A lot of being alive is touching,
delicately grazing fingers, *may I have more.*

Four seconds before the end of the world,
and I'm telling you:
this is how we've always done it.
We've always held each other,
thinking we can pull each other through,
across the divide.

Our innate drive to live,
amidst all other life,
following on from all those who have lived before,
in spite of the sacrifices that had to be made,
thinking that maybe,
this time,
it will be different.

Lily

If we could gather each atom of thought,
and bind them in a net,
if we could trace the seams of the universe,
and see it all at once,
the way it really is —
each ripple,
every fold —
then we would know the mind of God,
and it would be covered in moss,
and he would be laughing.
Because every second he is bent over,
laughing, and when he sleeps,
there is a static sound,
the way a city breathes:
the continuation of what we have created,
vibrating, clicking in our ears.
To create the universe as an afterthought,
and to give us the option to die,
to leave us floating through it all,
on a lily pad,
this universe, our pond,
adrift between each outer edge,
where even the water forgets its shape,
and we mistake its patterns
for meaning.

Database

We are modelers,
clay in our hands,
the atoms of reality
a database to mine.

Each moment pre-empts
its reception,
guessing its own expectations.
It leans into its echo,
unfinished, unfolding.

No single gene or neuron
binds the body to the world.
Each step, a domino,
tumbling through, in slow revolt,
until a breath is formed,
or, God help us, a thought.

Each succession, a scaffold we scale,
a pressure building
until we outpace the world we live in.
You are not your brain,
you are the state your mind can move into,
like something fragile and unreal.

Air rushing through a tunnel at high speed,
until suddenly,
nothing is left to channel it.

Tempus

I only have a couple of decades to say this.
I am scared.
I am hollowed out and wanting.
I am standing strong and shaking.
I have written across the days a singular song,
carried over by a wood pigeon's coo.

Independently of the things that change,
and the things that move,
I wish to be a constant.
As a child I would think —
if I were the grass,
or the clouds,
or that rock on the side of the road,
that tree over there —
the disloyalty of a moving thing,
still searching for her home.
I was looking for the permanent,
in a fugit world.
I want to stay.

Physics

We do not know of the gods,
except the laws that make up
the world in which we inhabit,
immediate or otherwise.

Who's to say that the magic of it
doesn't live up in the trees,
sketched into the underbelly
of roots that reach to one another
like hands under the earth.

That the mushroom does not bear witness
to the greater folds of universes,
trapped inside one another
like the curves of a seashell.

Join

What lurks in the quiet spaces in between?
We shape a world from the top down,
sending out silent predictions
of the shadows we hope to maybe meet.

Without the imagery of it,
we lean instead into the feel
of moments that stitch together
in our mind's eye,
each one threading softly into the next.

A tree
becomes a thing of reach
and power.
Its limbs parsed — each part,
fragments, one after another, after another —
until it sums into a whole,
and it is fighting for the light.
As am I,
hand outstretched toward a setting sun
that winks at the world
and fades.

Feather

We hold our lives up to the magnifying glass,
and find that there are only feathers,
the remnants of a living thing,
with no sight of the living.

How can we hold our choices in contempt,
when they are all that remain,
when the heart of the body
begins to breathe low.

We are shaped by steps taken
in the shadow of those that were not,
sketching one inevitable outline.
A river carving through earth,
led not by force,
but by the certainty of its own weight
to move through, because it must.

We steady ourselves
against each decision
with the ease of habit, the reassurance of time,
forgetting how dizzying they are
in their power to split a timeline apart.

Then we loosen our grip and let
those feathery fragments scatter,
each tracing its own quiet journey,
mapping what we cherish and what we shed.

In their drifting we discover
the soft contours of becoming,
lines of possibility unfurling
in the wake of every living choice.

A Guide to Being Strong

To wake up in earnest,
and reach for the glass
half empty,
and drink from it anyway,
every last drop.
To refill the kettle,
and wait for the French press
to brew, while counting the
thoughts that rumble through your
mind like a stampede.
To read, quietly, and for no
other reason than to pass the time.
To talk to the magpies at the window,
and give to them the shiny, silver things
you hold close to your heart,
and to watch them fly off
with the weight of them
between their small taloned claws.

Soundwave

This life I am building
is a steady echo, a wave
across the years
of the very elementary
particles we have come to know.
Shapeshifting, and yet,
I still recognise my voice
through every iteration,
as my own.

Printed in Dunstable, United Kingdom